HAYNES EXPLAINS
MARRIAGE

Owners' Workshop Manual

© Haynes Publishing • Written by **Boris Starling**

Published in October 2016

A catalogue record for this book is available from the British Library

ISBN 978 1 78521 104 1

Haynes Publishing, Sparkford, Yeovil,
Somerset BA22 7JJ, UK
Tel: +44 (0) 1963 440635
Website: www.haynes.com

Haynes North America, Inc.,
861 Lawrence Drive, Newbury Park,
California 91320, USA

Printed and bound in Malaysia

Cover image from Getty Images

Written by **Boris Starling**
Edited by **Louise McIntyre**
Designed by **Richard Parsons**

Safety first!

It's imperative to adhere to certain stringent safety measures with marriages, especially for the husband. The husband should assume that he's in the wrong unless he is in total and explicit agreement with his wife, and sometimes not even then. The following phrases signal imminent spousal explosion and should be treated with extreme caution:

'It's your decision.'
'No, nothing's wrong.'
'Do what you want.'
'We need to talk.'
'I don't want to talk about it.'
'Are you listening to me?'

Working facilities

Optimum working facilities for a marriage vary widely. Some couples may find that a small apartment is best practice. Some may prefer something the size of a stately home with a dining table sufficiently long as to merit binoculars and an intercom system. Some may prefer a marriage of even greater distance, with for example one party in London and the other in New York. Kitchens should be either too small to allow room for thrown crockery or sufficiently large to enable taking evasive action against same.

Contents

Introduction

It's divided into two parts: the wedding and the marriage. As the old adage goes, wedding is a word and marriage is a sentence. Weddings are by far the easier bit of the two, even if you might not necessarily believe that halfway through the reception when both sets of relatives have had a skinful, the DJ's just put on Elton John's *Saturday Night's Alright For Fighting* and it's about to kick off like an *Eastenders* Christmas.

Think of the difference between a wedding and a marriage as that between choosing a car and living with that car: all showroom fresh and gleaming bright to start with, but what about a few years down the line? Will it still be running smoothly and have the warm patina of comfortable use, or will it be scuffed, worn, torn and neglected?

It's easy to think that the wedding needs all the hard work and the marriage will take care of itself. The opposite is usually true.

About this manual

The aim of this manual is to help you get the best value from your Marriage. It can do this in several ways. It can help you (a) decide what work must be done and (b) tackle this work yourself, though you may choose to have much of it performed by external contractors such as the local pizza delivery company, the garage that sells just-on-the-right-side-of-crappy flowers, or (failing those) your local Relate counsellor. Beware: every marriage has a point beyond which outsourcing becomes no longer cost-effective.

The manual has drawings and descriptions to show the function and layout of the various components. Tasks are described in a logical order so that even a novice can do the work, which should prove useful if you've ever forgotten whose turn it is to put the bins out, stack the dishwasher, empty the dishwasher or fix that wonky shelf in the spare bedroom which *I'VE BEEN ASKING YOU TO DO FOR SIX MONTHS WHY DO YOU NEVER EVER, EVER LISTEN?*

Dimensions, weights and capacities

Kerb weight (average)
Bride (after intense dieting) 52kg
Groom (after less intense dieting): 82kg

Speeches (length)
Bride's father .... 3 mins
Groom .... 7 mins
Best man .... 142 mins

Maximum acceleration
Of bride towards groom when
she sees him talking to his ex: .... 0–60 in 1.2 secs
Of pissed relatives towards
an inevitable fight: .... 20 mins +/- 5 mins

Maximum speed and acceleration
First thing in morning .... 1.5mph. 0–maximum: 45 mins
When angry .... 7434 mph. 0–60: 0.000005 sec

Engine
Made of .... 49% alcohol, 26% bonhomie, 17% flirting
.... between best man and maid of honour,
.... 8% fixed grins for official photos.
Bore .... Take your pick.
Stroke .... In the bushes past midnight once drink
.... has been taken. AKA 'party hands'.
Power.. Resides with whoever's paying for the
.... whole thing, usually.
Torque .... Lots and lots of talking (see 'speeches').
Redline .... When That Waiter Who Thinks He's Too
.... Good For This gives you lip.

PART ONE:
THE WEDDING

Making an offer

To any man before proposing: you should be nervous. You won't ask many more important questions in your life (except perhaps 'anyone got a spare Springsteen ticket?') A man who isn't nervous is either:

a) Lying
b) Stoned
c) Three or four marriages down already.

If you feel you need a little Dutch courage before the off, you're not the first and you won't be the last. Two drinks maximum, though. This is no time to slur your words, forget her name or drop the ring down the nearest drain. Two drinks was traditionally the sweet spot for darts players before they got all sponsor-friendly and teetotal. If it's good enough for Jocky Wilson and Eric Bristow….

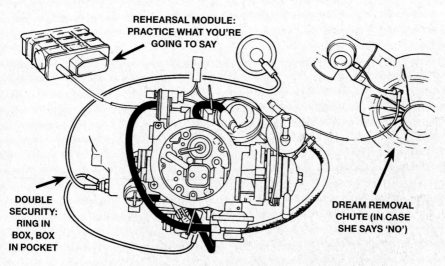

REHEARSAL MODULE: PRACTICE WHAT YOU'RE GOING TO SAY

DOUBLE SECURITY: RING IN BOX, BOX IN POCKET

DREAM REMOVAL CHUTE (IN CASE SHE SAYS 'NO')

FIG 3•1 **CHECK YOUR WIRING AND MAKE SURE NO SCREWS ARE LOOSE**

⚠ Popping the question

Thou shalt apprise her father (and mother too, if appropriate) of your intentions beforehand. Asking the old man's permission is a bit old hat now – she's not his possession any more than she'll be yours – but most fathers will still appreciate being informed.

Thou shalt think like a lawyer. No, not how many hours you can reasonably bill your client. This: don't ask the question unless you know the answer. If you don't know the answer, you shouldn't be asking.

Thou shalt remember the first essential part of the proposal: drop to one knee. Yes, it's cheesy. Yes, her friends will ask if you did. Yes, she'll hate it if she can't tell them that you did.

Thou shalt remember the second essential part of the proposal: take the ring out of the box and put it on her finger. See above re cheesiness and friends asking.

Thou shalt remember the third essential part of the proposal: whatever else you say, end your speech with the phrase 'will you marry me?' Not least because it may be the last time she listens to a word you say.

Thou shalt not involve other members of the public. Having a flash mob of singers disguised as a roadworks crew, or spelling it out on the big screen at a sports stadium, may look good on YouTube, but it will just put her on the spot and make it more about you than her, you rampant narcissist.

Thou shalt not involve animals. Getting a cat or dog to carry the ring sounds great right up until said animal swallows the ring, at which point you need either a decent insurance policy or a clothes peg and a pair of industrial-strength rubber gloves.

Thou shalt not do it on her birthday, as that just looks like a cheap attempt at getting out of buying her a birthday present. Same goes for Christmas Day.

Thou shalt not do it anywhere from which you can't escape if she says no – the start of a long-haul flight, for example. Awkward.

***Thou shalt not* do it just after a positive pregnancy test. Practical, yes. Romantic, no.**

The dashboard

**'Planning this wedding:
I'd like to be more involved'
said no groom ever.**

**'Planning this wedding:
it's really easy and stress-free'
said no bride ever.**

There's a reason that professional wedding planners make a decent living – working out the details of even a small ceremony can quickly spiral from itchy-coochy-coo wouldn't-this-be-lovely ideas to hair-tearing vein-popping screaming matches about floral centrepieces. Having a wedding planner is like trusting your directions to a sat-nav: not only are you outsourcing to a professional but you also have someone to blame other than each other if it all goes wrong.

If you think hiring a professional is expensive, wait till you hire an amateur.

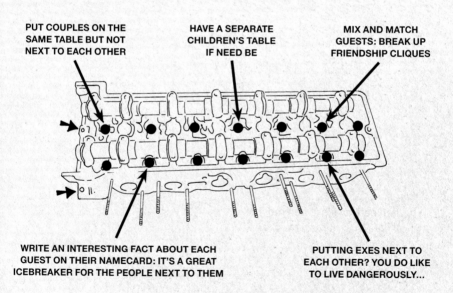

PUT COUPLES ON THE SAME TABLE BUT NOT NEXT TO EACH OTHER

HAVE A SEPARATE CHILDREN'S TABLE IF NEED BE

MIX AND MATCH GUESTS: BREAK UP FRIENDSHIP CLIQUES

WRITE AN INTERESTING FACT ABOUT EACH GUEST ON THEIR NAMECARD: IT'S A GREAT ICEBREAKER FOR THE PEOPLE NEXT TO THEM

PUTTING EXES NEXT TO EACH OTHER? YOU DO LIKE TO LIVE DANGEROUSLY...

FIG 3•2 **SQUARING THE CIRCLE: SEATING PLANS**

⚠ Wedding planning tips

If your budget and/or preferences don't stretch to having a third party inserting themselves in the middle of your happy day (include mother-in-law joke of your choice here), you'll want to do it all yourselves.

1) All those little details you spend hours discussing – none of your guests are going to notice them. Literally, not a single guest. A good wedding needs much less than you may think: a couple in love, good food and booze, dancing, and, er, that's it. It doesn't need wedding programmes on parchment made from the hide of Armenian yaks or chairs hand-carved from Mauritanian oak by the finest artisanal carpenters in Provence.

2) There are two groups of people: those you invite and those who'll never speak to you again. And the quickest way to cut costs is to cut the number of guests. Easier said than done, of course. Try to get married early in life (when most of your friends are still single) or late (when they're divorced). Getting married in the middle means most of your friends will be paired off, which effectively halves the number you can invite.

3) Try not to split groups of friends – invite everyone in your office or none of them, for example. If you must split groups, make sure the non-attendees are the majority: they'll feel less offended and those who did make the cut will feel more special.

4) Don't just invite people to one part of the celebration. No guest feels great turning up at 8pm for the evening do when everyone else has been going for five hours and can barely remember their own name.

IT'S A TABLECLOTH, NOT THE TURIN SHROUD

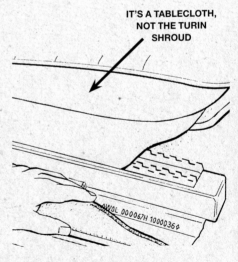

FIG 3•3 **DON'T SWEAT THE SMALL STUFF**

Last stop before the motorway

Somewhere out there, probably not far from the Loch Ness Monster, is the much-rumoured but mythical creature – The Man Who Enjoyed A Stag Night. He is further thought to have a female counterpart, The Woman Who Enjoyed A Hen Night, but this has never been confirmed.

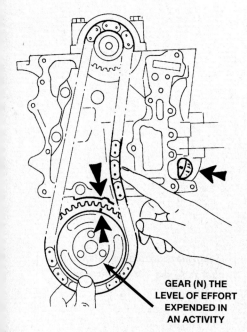

GEAR (N) THE LEVEL OF EFFORT EXPENDED IN AN ACTIVITY

FIG 3•4 **PUTTING THE SQUEEZE ON. PRIME TARGET: YOUR WALLET**

Let's get this out there...

Stag and hen nights are frightful. They used to be OK – basically a night with your mates in the pub the night before the wedding, which often meant a bleary-eyed bride and groom but no worse than that. Now they:

a) cost money you don't have
b) take time you'd rather spend doing something – anything – else
c) involve travel to a place you'd never visit in a million years otherwise
d) burden you with activities that you've inevitably done before on previous stag/hen nights (paintballing/bull-running/quadbiking for the stags, spa sessions/burlesque lessons/cocktail mixing for the hens)
e) involve so much drinking that it doesn't matter where you are
f) are full of people you either see quite enough of as it is or you've never met before and, the wedding apart, will never meet again.

So here's a list of stag/hen night do's and don'ts

a) Don't. Just don't.

Stag/hen night do's and don'ts

Oh, alright then. If you really have to go on a stag or hen night – and at some stage you really will have to unless you're a hermit with literally no friends and weapons-grade halitosis – then remember the following:

1) What goes on tour stays on tour. No social media posts during the trip, and a mafia-style omertà when you return home. This can be to avoid indiscretions making their way to the wider world, or it can just be to make it sound more interesting than it was.

2) Don't go too far. Shave nothing that won't grow back, apply no tattoos that can't be easily removed, inflict no scars that won't fade.

3) Don't jib. Go with the majority, do whatever they want to do – drink shots, lap dancing, whatever. Think collective responsibility.

4) If you're a bunch of lairy men who are let into an Amsterdam nightclub en masse, there's probably a reason for that, and the reason is not unconnected to the fact the club's called 'Cockring'.

5) If you're going abroad, check the exchange rate beforehand. The man who airily plonks his Amex card behind the bar and says 'it's so cheap, I'll cover this' is the man whose wife gets a call early the following morning asking whether the £8,000 spent at Pussy Palace in Reykjavik is a legitimate transaction.

6) If you go to a British provincial town beginning with 'B' – Bangor, Bognor, Bournemouth, Blackpool, Brighton – your hostel will be fetid, your curry will be terrible, and weekend engineering works will make your return train journey take seven hours longer than usual.

WARNING

BEWARE There's always a bossy member of the party (Stagzilla/Henzilla) who takes charge of the kitty, is forever on the phone asking why the taxis are three minutes late, and so on. If you can't identify this person, you may well be that person. Don't be that person.

Sealing the deal

The first four questions anyone asks about a wedding are:

a) How did the bride look?
b) What were the speeches like?
c) What was their first song?
d) Can I see the photos?

How did the bride look?
Don't ask a man what the bride's dress was like. If you're lucky, he'll have noticed it was white. Other than that, he won't have a clue, even (or perhaps especially) if he's the groom. Ask any woman who was there, and you'll get chapter and verse on the neckline, train, topper, beads, sleeves....

What were the speeches like?
There's nothing worse than the amateur comedian who goes on. And on. And on. Forty-five minutes is bad. Five minutes is good. 'Just A Minute' – 60 seconds with no hesitation, deviation or repetition – is even better. Be short and be sweet: something amusing but heartfelt about the couple always gets bigger laughs than a well-crafted but irrelevant joke. Practice beforehand, preferably in front of two people (one male, one female) whose judgement you trust. If they tell you to take something out, do it. Use index cards as prompts, but don't type the speech out in full or else you risk reading it in a monotone.

BE PREPARED FOR EMERGENCY SEAMSTRESSING

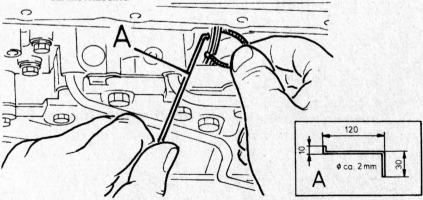

FIG 3•5 **FINE ADJUSTMENT: THE ART OF MAKING IT MEMORABLE**

What was their first song?

Unless you fancy yourselves as Fred and Ginger, John Travolta and Uma Thurman from *Pulp Fiction*, or an audition tape for *Strictly*, keep your first song short. A verse and a chorus is enough time to dance alone, then get everyone else on the floor. Make sure the early music is oldie-friendly before your elderly guests slip away (unless your nan likes to throw shapes on the dancefloor to David Guetta, in which case upload the video to YouTube and start monetising the views: this wedding's not paying for itself, you know). The groom or best man should dance with any single old lady there: it will absolutely make her night.

Can I see the photos?

Although everybody now has a smartphone, you still can't beat a proper, professional wedding photographer. Go through with them beforehand the basic shots you need: you'd be surprised how many can get missed during the day. Make sure the photographer gets lots of you relaxed (yeah, right) and larking about too: these are the ones that often capture a wedding's flavour more than stiff family portraits with everyone keeping a lid on their own personal *Game Of Thrones*-style clan grudges.

Other tips

Write your own wedding vows. It makes it much more personal. Grooms – don't waste your time trying to get her to 'obey' alongside loving and honouring. No chance, son.

The happy couple should circulate. Everyone's there for you: try to talk to them all.

Mix up the seating plan: don't just put people with those they know.

Responsibility for young children rests with their parents, not whoever happens to be nearest. This isn't some fancy continental zonal marking system.

Don't expect everything to go to plan. It won't. And when it doesn't, nine times out of ten it won't matter (unless it's the booze running out, which is only marginally less apocalyptic than the arrival of the Four Horsemen).

That new car smell

Let's be honest. Most grooms would happily go to the nearest Premier Inn for their honeymoon, since they only have one thing on their mind and it doesn't entail leaving the room (though if the Premier Inn adverts are anything to go by you might always find Lenny Henry popping up in your bed, which would put the sturdiest fellow off his stride). Luckily most brides are more sensible, and hence head for somewhere with lots of sun, sand, sea and of course everything else beginning with 's'.

Enjoy your honeymoon

Make sure you enjoy every minute of your honeymoon, because the moment the wheels of your plane touch down at Heathrow (inevitably on a grey and rainy morning), you are back to life, back to reality and most of all entering a new phase. Wedding is now over, gone, history. Welcome to marriage. You will still have plenty of memories of your honeymoon. They will come every month on your credit card bill.

⚠ Things to bring...

☑ Lingerie. If you don't make the best use of it now, you never will. This is no time to be shy, and not just in the bedroom either. Almost everyone is happy to see a newly married couple, and just the word 'honeymoon' may lead to special treatment, airline upgrades, more luxurious hotel rooms and so on.

☑ A bag to half-inch all those complimentary high-end hotel products. Yes, they'll probably end up sitting unused on the shelf of your bathroom for the next decade and a half, but **THEY'RE STILL FREE**.

☑ Half as many clothes as you originally packed. Your husband won't notice anyway. He may be pleasantly surprised that he has more than 10% of the suitcase to himself, but he almost certainly won't mention this for fear that it's some sort of administrative error or something.

Honeymoon (n): the last holiday a man has before he starts working for a new boss.

⚠ Things NOT to bring...

✗ Other people. No friends, no family, no children. A honeymoon should be just the two of you, especially as it's liable to take place during the period you still enjoy being with each other (see, er, MARRIAGE). Otherwise it's just a holiday.

....

✗ An alarm clock. Go to bed late, sleep late. Eat breakfast at 11, lunch at 4 and supper at 10. It won't be long before you're back to the usual routine of grabbing a cappuccino to go before dawn and a soggy takeaway on the way home that evening.

✗ A wifi password. Work e-mails can wait, as can all the #honeymoon social media posts, which will in any case annoy your friends sooner than they'd admit. This may be the last time for a long time you ever get to be alone and carefree. Don't share it with the world. However, if you absolutely must, then one artfully filtered tropical sunset with a champagne glass in the foreground. Just one. But at least be honest #kingandqueenofsmuggery, #honeymoonersandlovingit, #lifesabeach, #doyouallhateusyet.

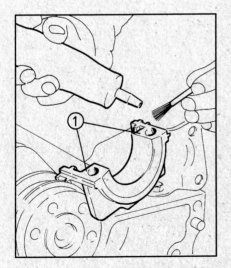

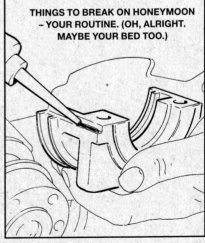

THINGS TO BREAK ON HONEYMOON – YOUR ROUTINE. (OH, ALRIGHT. MAYBE YOUR BED TOO.)

FIG 3•6 **LEAVE YOUR HOBBIES AT HOME**

PART TWO: THE MARRIAGE

Road tax

Money. You may remember it from when you were single. It might be the root of all evil. It's certainly the root of most marital beefs, more so even than 'why is Tracy from Accounts texting you at 11.30pm?' and 'well, if you'd only do what I asked then I wouldn't have to nag, would I?'

Whoever said money can't buy you love was in the wrong income bracket. She says he earns too little; he says she spends too much. Most married couples know how to handle money: they could just do with handling it a little less often. And if as many married couples were as deeply in love as they are in debt, divorce rates would be even lower than interest rates.

Wealth (n): any income that is at least £500 more per annum than that of one's wife's sister's husband.

THE AMOUNT OF MONEY YOU HAVE

THE AMOUNT OF MONEY YOU NEED

5°

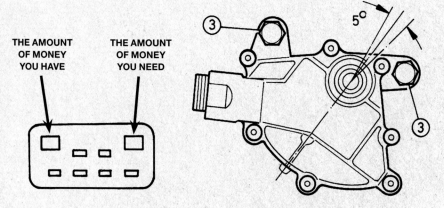

FIG 3•7 **NEVER QUITE ENOUGH: THE MARRIAGE MONEY-MAKING MACHINE**

Dealing with money issues

1) There's no sexy way to say it: you need a household budget. Many couples have a joint account for household bills – mortgage/rent, utilities, food etc. – and maintain separate ones for their own use, which avoids arguments about him spending too much on video games or her on a new outfit. In theory, at least.

2) Assign roles to whoever fits them best. The belief that the husband should automatically handle long-term planning and investments while the wife deals with the household budget went out of fashion at roughly the same time as the zoot suit. If a man can remember the scores of every FA Cup final back to 1973 then he has the detail-focused OCD to scour out supermarket vouchers and save the pennies.

3) Don't keep money secrets from your partner. Tell them about all your debts, loans, child-support payments and so on. If they don't know about your child-support payments as they don't know about the children being supported… well, make sure your partner isn't within reach of sharp objects when you drop this one. Same goes in the case of you already being married*.
(*not necessarily applicable in Saudi Arabia or Utah).

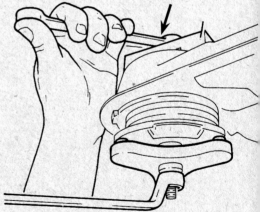

MINI METAL DETECTORS CAN REACH HARD-TO-ACCESS AREAS

FIG 3•8 **LOOK FOR MONEY IN EVERY NOOK AND CRANNY, NOT JUST DOWN THE BACK OF THE SOFA**

Maths question for men: You have £20. Your wife has £5. How much does your wife have? Answer: £25.

Depreciation (men)

Remember those little habits your other half had that you found so endearing when you first started going out? A tenner says it's now exactly those habits that set your teeth on edge and make you not just homicidal but positively genocidal. Some women even object to the way their husband breathes (or perhaps just to the fact that he breathes, let alone how he does it). You, of course, have no annoying habits at all. Not one.

Marriage basically lets you annoy one special person for the rest of your life. Here are the most annoying habits of married men.

1. Anything bodily

Picking his nose, picking his teeth, breaking wind. Especially in bed. If a man rolls half onto his side in bed, pauses for a moment and then gathers the duvet tightly round himself, he has just farted, and under an obscure clause included in the 1828 Offences Against The Person Act and never repealed, you have the right to kill him.

2. Selective listening

You're talking to him. He's nodding and going 'mm-hmm' occasionally, but he's watching TV or looking at his phone. Tell him you're having an affair with George Clooney. He won't hear. Or he'll think you said you're going to the fair with Wayne Rooney.

3. Untidiness

Look at this one from his point of view. The floor's a big area, and it's a bit of a waste if all we ever do is walk on it. Wouldn't it look better with a bit of mud here and some dirty clothes there? What's that? The laundry basket? That thing that looks like a giant lobster pot? Wow. Never knew that.

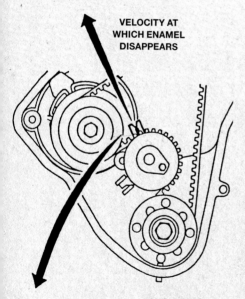

VELOCITY AT WHICH ENAMEL DISAPPEARS

FIG 3•9 **THE BRUXISM MECHANISM: TEETH GRINDING BORNE OF FRUSTRATION**

4. Snoring

Doesn't matter whether it's a soft wheezing, a sharply revving chainsaw, a fleet of pneumatic drills or a herd of elephants thundering across the savannah: at three in the morning, snoring is snoring, and any snoring is too loud. The worst thing about snoring, of course, is not just that you're awake – it's that he, the perpetrator, the bringer of this vile noise pollution, is sleeping through all this as happy as bloody Larry. And then he has the temerity to start...

5. Waking you up when you're snoring

Say no more. Only made worse by when he pretends he didn't and feigns sleep. Just about plausible if you're married to Mr Tickle with his extendable arms. Not otherwise. Like him, you will refuse to admit you were snoring. Like him, you may resort to recording the sound on your phone. Like him, you will refuse to admit that the recording is of you, before considering that any possible alternative is much less palatable.

6. Not knowing where anything is

Especially applicable in the kitchen. Never seems to apply to the DVD collection, strangely. A close cousin of his inability to find something in the fridge even when looking straight at it.

7. Losing his keys

How come your keys are surgically attached to you, but he could lose his in the middle of an empty tennis court? 'I had them just here, I'm sure,' he'll say. 'Where could they be?' He looks everywhere, messing up perfectly tidy room after perfectly tidy room, as the search becomes ever more outlandish and unlikely. Why? – how? – could they possibly have got into the freezer?

8. Leaving the toilet seat up

Especially because the now exposed white porcelain rim is very visibly unforgiving of men whose aim is less than laser accurate.

9. Leaving the toilet paper roll empty

Or even worse, leaving it with a mockingly inadequate single sheet of paper left on the cardboard. There is no circumstance in which this is anything other than hideously selfish. If you're desperate to use the toilet, you'll have to use up precious seconds going to get a new roll from the cupboard.

Enjoy long walks – especially when taken by those who annoy you

Depreciation (women)

And, in the interests of gender equality, the most annoying habits of married women. Yes, I know there were nine for the men but there are only five here. (I'm not as dumb as I look.)

1. Endless talking

More specifically, what men of a certain age would call 'dollywaffle'. Must you and your girlfriends share absolutely every detail of your lives with each other? And when you're telling your husband something, you don't have to give it a half-hour preamble. If he says 'can you just get to the important bit?' it's not

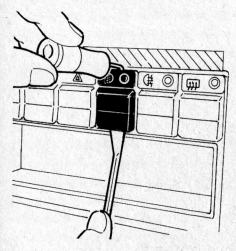

FIG 3•10 **INSERT CAREFULLY IN ORDER TO GET A WORD IN EDGEWAYS**

because he's not interested: it's because he is interested but fears the Reaper will come for him first if you don't get a shift on.

2. The waterworks

Men cry at only a handful of things – their football team losing, being kicked shatteringly hard in the crown jewels, the end of *Toy Story 3*, and… er, that's about it. They don't know how to deal with crying women, other than to do whatever it takes to stop them crying. They do suspect that this might very well be the point of the crying in the first place.

3. Indecision

This top or that one? These shoes or those? Yes, that outfit looks nice. Yes, that outfit looks nice too. No, I'm not just saying that, I mean it, it's not a zero-sum game. Please just choose something and let's go out otherwise the party will be over before we get there. What do you mean, you need more time?

4. Nagging

Though to be honest after a while it's just white noise.

5. Refusing to order pudding

And then eating all of his.

⚠️ What the wife means

What the wife says	What the wife means
We need to talk	You need to listen
Nothing's wrong	You're in a whole world of pain
I'm fine	I expect you to be a mind reader
I have nothing to wear	Three full wardrobes but no power of decision
Her? She's more of a man's woman	All my female friends hate her and I will kill you if you so much as smile at her
Do whatever you want	Do exactly what I want
I need space	Get out now and do not come back till I text
You don't have to	You absolutely have to
We'll talk about this later	You'd better start grovelling
I forgive you	I will use this against you
You've still got a sense of humour	You're letting yourself go.
Do you think she's pretty?	Tell me I'm pretty and make sure you mean it
Maybe	No
No	Not till hell freezes over
We need	I want
Do you love me?	I'm going to suggest something expensive
How much do you love me?	I'm about to make you really angry
Are you listening to me?	You're dead
I'm sorry	You'll be sorry
What did you say?	Last chance to change your mind
I'm not yelling!	They can hear me in China
Only when you have a moment	Do it. Now. Right now.
Your friends don't like me	I don't like your friends
How do you know her?	Did you ever sleep with her?

Crash test ratings

Arguments are part and parcel of marriage, and beware the couple that doesn't argue: they are storing up resentments that may prove far more damaging further down the line.

Winning an argument

Winning an argument isn't important (unless you're a barrister); trying to solve what caused the argument in the first place is important. Being kind is more important than being right. Keep your words as free from bitterness as possible, as that way they'll taste better when you have to eat them. And what could be a civilised discussion at lunchtime can easily

become a screaming match late at night when both parties are knackered.

Money aside (see 'road tax'), things most reliably guaranteed to spark off marital conflict are small and electronic. (No, not from Ann Summers.)

The remote control

Wars for land and resources have been waged with less ferocity and cunning than those fought across the world every day for control of the remote. Yes, you can have two TVs, not to mention watching programmes on your laptop and/or via catch-up, though for many married couples watching TV together still counts as spending time together – but what to watch? Who gets to decide what to watch live and what to catch up with later?

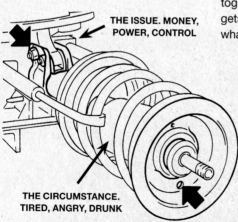

THE ISSUE. MONEY, POWER, CONTROL

THE CIRCUMSTANCE. TIRED, ANGRY, DRUNK

FIG 3•11 **PRESSURE POINTS: HOW TO START AN ARGUMENT EVERY TIME**

Compromise today and reap the rewards tomorrow, but remember that all marriage brownie points have a strict expiry date: use them or lose them.

⚠ Thermostat perpetual motion

Even the couple who are a perfect match may find that their metabolisms are not. Temperature up or down? Put on more layers or take them off? Warm blood or cold?

This is not just a thermostat: it is a fight for our very souls. Which is why a man who cannot hear a dog barking the house down at four in the morning can, at five miles in a high wind, hear the click of a thermostat being minutely adjusted.

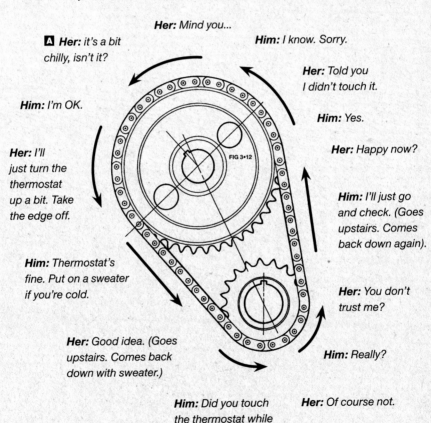

Her: Mind you...

A **Her:** it's a bit chilly, isn't it?

Him: I know. Sorry.

Him: I'm OK.

Her: Told you I didn't touch it.

Him: Yes.

Her: I'll just turn the thermostat up a bit. Take the edge off.

Her: Happy now?

Him: I'll just go and check. (Goes upstairs. Comes back down again).

Him: Thermostat's fine. Put on a sweater if you're cold.

Her: You don't trust me?

Her: Good idea. (Goes upstairs. Comes back down with sweater.)

Him: Really?

Him: Did you touch the thermostat while you were up there?

Her: Of course not.

FIG 3•12

Pillow torque

There are enough aphorisms about marriage and sex to keep comedians in work for years.

a) Marriage: like prison, but without the sex.

b) Sex in marriage is like medicine: three times a day for the first week and then once a day for the next week, by which time the condition will have cleared up and you can stop altogether.

c) Sex when you're married is like going to the 7-Eleven: there's not much variety, but at three in the morning it's always there.

And so on. When it comes to sex, the familiarity of marriage can breed complacency if not outright contempt (and if it does breed contempt, at least make sure you have stilettos and a safe word). *Fifty Shades Of Grey* has made all that stuff much more acceptable. But do remember the safe word. Forgetting that is worse than forgetting your computer password.

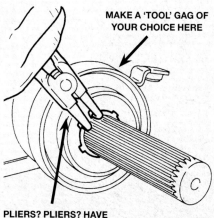

MAKE A 'TOOL' GAG OF YOUR CHOICE HERE

PLIERS? PLIERS? HAVE YOU NO MERCY?

FIG 3•13 **PREPARING THE SLIDER JOINT**

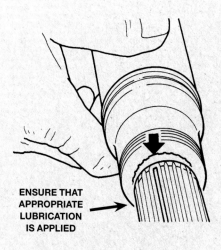

ENSURE THAT APPROPRIATE LUBRICATION IS APPLIED

FIG 3•14 **MASTER SPLINE ON SLIDER JOINT**

WARNING

'My wife is a sex object. Every time I ask her for sex, she objects.' – Les Dawson

⚠ Keeping things fresh

1) Make sure you go on a date at least once a week. It doesn't have to be wildly expensive or terrifically exciting – a cheap restaurant or a movie will do – but it does have to be time for you to get dressed up a little and be together without worrying about work, the children, bills or imminent world war.

2) Make yourself attractive. Don't take it for granted that your spouse will keep fancying you just because you're married. Keep making the effort you used to make in the early days. Work out. Buy new clothes from time to time. If you have a beard, shave it off (men only). If you don't have a beard, grow one (ditto).

3) Make the other person feel good. Give them a back rub. Hide love notes for them to find. Buy them flowers (remove the 'Texaco Special Offer' sticker before handing them over) or pick them yourself (bucolic country lane good, Buckingham Palace garden bad).

4) Initiate random sex in odd places, such as by the freezer (better at home than in Morrison's). Wake them up in the small hours like you used to do in your early days together. Don't say 'I can hear someone moving around downstairs' or 'did you leave the iron on?'

'WHAT DO YOU MEAN, YOU'VE FORGOTTEN THE SAFE WORD?'

TWIST HARD, TIGHTEN NUT – HONESTLY, THIS STUFF WRITES ITSELF

FIG 3•15 **MORE TOYS THAN HAMLEY'S. (NOT QUITE THE SAME TYPE, GRANTED)**

The spare tyre

In dietary terms, getting married is generally very good for a man. He's liable to come across foodstuffs which until now have remained alien to him. Such foodstuffs are mainly green in colour, though sometimes they can be orange or purple too. These are called vegetables. They will not hurt him. If he's feeling especially adventurous, he can move onto their close cousins, fruit. If his wife asks him whether a tomato is a vegetable or a fruit, he should ignore her. She is only trying to confuse him.

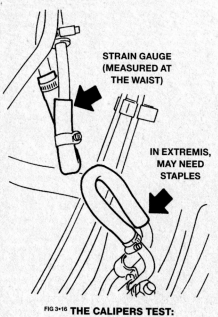

STRAIN GAUGE
(MEASURED AT
THE WAIST)

IN EXTREMIS,
MAY NEED
STAPLES

FIG 3•16 **THE CALIPERS TEST:
PINCHING MORE THAN AN INCH**

For women, marriage can be more hazardous to the waistline. Gone are the healthy low-fat meals for one you used to rustle up: now you cook for two, and it's all too easy to let your portions match his even though he's bigger and needs more calories than you do. Gone are nights in the gym in favour of takeaways, restaurants, dinner parties and booze. When you're comfortable with your man, you don't mind if you put on a bit of weight – until you do, at which point he'll start complaining that he never sees you anymore as you're always in the gym.

The modern husband

Modern metrosexual men know their way round a kitchen – they all think they're Jamie Oliver. So outsourcing the cooking to them a few nights a week sounds like a good plan, right? Wrong. They'll cook for the two of you the same way you cook for the two of you – with his needs in mind. If you cooked with your needs in mind, you'd never hear the end of his bleating about rabbit food, what time is McDonald's open till, this is worse than the Irish potato famine, and on and on and on.

Basically, to keep to pre-marriage weight you need the willpower of Gandhi (though probably not the loincloth or the glasses).

⚠ The very hungry husband

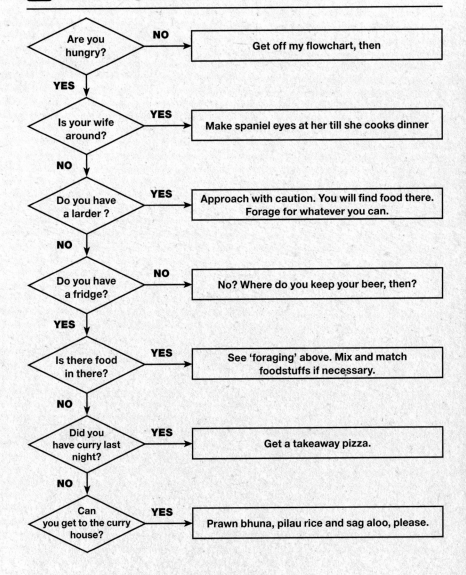

Are you hungry? — NO → Get off my flowchart, then

YES ↓

Is your wife around? — YES → Make spaniel eyes at her till she cooks dinner

NO ↓

Do you have a larder? — YES → Approach with caution. You will find food there. Forage for whatever you can.

NO ↓

Do you have a fridge? — NO → No? Where do you keep your beer, then?

YES ↓

Is there food in there? — YES → See 'foraging' above. Mix and match foodstuffs if necessary.

NO ↓

Did you have curry last night? — YES → Get a takeaway pizza.

NO ↓

Can you get to the curry house? — YES → Prawn bhuna, pilau rice and sag aloo, please.

Backseat drivers

It's amazing the International Olympic Committee hasn't added The In-Law Visit to their list of approved sports. Having the in-laws to stay is a perfect fit for the Olympic Games: you need many hours of meticulous preparation, you are judged on even the smallest thing, and you will almost certainly need illegal drugs to get through the process in one piece. The Olympics, however, take place only every four years. Lucky indeed is the spouse who can keep her in-laws' visiting to a similar schedule.

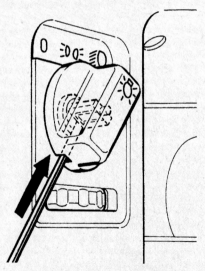

FIG 3•17 **IN-LAW SELECTOR SWITCH. THREE SETTINGS – OFF; 'IF YOU SAY SO'; 'THAT'S VERY INTERESTING.'**

Before the visit

When your in-laws ask what is a good time for them to come (and count yourself lucky if they do ask rather than simply descend on you as though this was some state visit), resist the temptation to reply: 'Never? How does never work for you?' Short-term gain, maybe, but long-term pain. You'll just be putting off the day of reckoning.

Try to have them come at a time when you're not insanely busy, and at a time when they can help out as much as possible: not only will this reduce stress on you, but it will give them plenty to do while they're there. If your house is big enough, put them in a guest room. If it's not, a nearby hotel is good. A distant hotel is even better.

Sit down with your husband before the in-laws arrive and work out how to handle any likely problems that could arise during the visit. Make a 'top ten' list if need be. Then another ten. And another ten. You may need alcohol while doing this. Agree on how to handle any such problems.*

(*Get him to deal with them all. They're his parents, aren't they?)

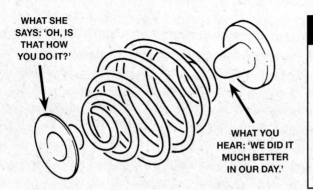

WHAT SHE SAYS: 'OH, IS THAT HOW YOU DO IT?'

WHAT YOU HEAR: 'WE DID IT MUCH BETTER IN OUR DAY.'

FIG 3•18 **THE M-I-L™ BRAIN SCRAMBLER**

WARNING

It's important to retain a soft spot for your mother-in-law. About halfway down the garden between the shed and the compost heap is ideal.

During the visit

Treat your in-laws like your children: keep them occupied, tire them out, ply them with alcohol. (Well, two out of three ain't bad.)

Fathers-in-law can be excellent handymen around the house, taking less than a day to fix all the things your husband hasn't managed in six months. (Like male-pattern baldness, the DIY gene often seems to skip a generation.)

Mothers-in-law can help in the kitchen. (Your in-laws are liable to have more rigid gender roles than you and your husband might do, unless they met in a hippy commune.) If you have children, letting your in-laws spend time with their grandchildren can make everyone happy.

Don't be afraid to have friends round: it can break up the time and stimulate more conversation.

Choose which particular friends wisely, of course. Charming Crispin who took one for the team at your wedding by sitting next to an old dear is good. Suzie Shit-Stirrer who likes to whip up trouble and will allude to what you've said about your in-laws in private is bad.

Your mother-in-law will almost certainly hold trenchant views on any or all of the following: how clean your house is, how good the furniture is, how comfortable her bed is, how hot the water is, how well- or badly behaved your children are, how lucky you are to be married to her son, your cooking, your washing, your looks, your personality. If it all gets too much, pretend not to speak English.

After the visit

Wine. Chocolates. Bath. Bed. Because you're worth it.

Differentials

When you get married, two become one and 'I' becomes 'we'. You combine your finances, possessions, love and life goals. It's tempting to think that you have to spend every waking, non-working hour together when you're married, especially when that time is precious.

But it's easy to lose the part of yourself that makes you unique, and to unconsciously let go of the things you love to do just because your spouse doesn't do them. It won't be long before both of you start to want some space. Just because you're together forever doesn't mean you have to be forever together. Domesticity is just as big a killer of marital bliss as distance, perhaps more so. And having healthy time apart can head off the temptation to have some unhealthy time apart.

Paul Newman once said: 'For people who have as little in common as Joanne [Woodward] and myself, we have an uncommonly good marriage. Husbands and wives should have separate interests, cultivate different sets of friends and not impose on the other. You can't spend a lifetime breathing down each other's necks.' And if it's good enough for Butch Cassidy, Fast Eddie and Cool Hand Luke, it's good enough for you.

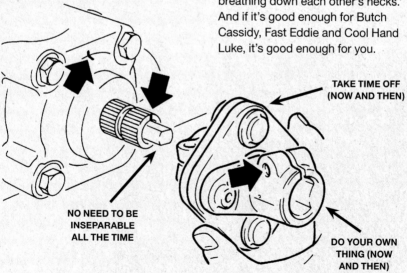

TAKE TIME OFF (NOW AND THEN)

NO NEED TO BE INSEPARABLE ALL THE TIME

DO YOUR OWN THING (NOW AND THEN)

FIG 3•19 **TEMPORARY UNCOUPLING**

⚠ Time spent apart

1) If your husband plays golf every Saturday, then you should – actually, if your husband plays golf every Saturday you should reconsider your entire existence, since golf is the most achingly tedious of all 'sports.' But given you've now gone through with the ceremony and everything, it's probably best to take less drastic measures. Do something of your own – go running, go riding, go back to sleep.

2) Have a good, tight group of girlfriends with whom you can laugh, kvetch and bitch about your husbands. If nothing else, you'll come away convinced that yours isn't so bad after all.

3) Your interests might be different, but that doesn't mean they can't be compatible – that is, they don't compete with or interfere with each other.

If all else fails, heed the words of Henny Youngman: 'Some people ask the secret of our long marriage. We take time to go to a restaurant two times a week. A little candlelight, dinner, soft music and dancing. She goes Tuesdays, I go Fridays.'

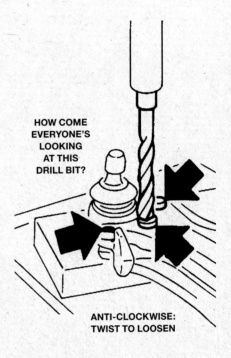

HOW COME EVERYONE'S LOOKING AT THIS DRILL BIT?

ANTI-CLOCKWISE: TWIST TO LOOSEN

FIG 3•20 **RELEASING THE TENSION**

You'll often find a couple who have never considered divorce, but you'll rarely find one who have never considered murder.

Aerodynamics and drag

Even the best marriage can feel stale now and then. To avoid drag, consider the following from time to time:

Moving house
Within reason, of course: moving house is widely seen as the most stressful thing in life after death and divorce, and if you do it too often it may lead to one or both of those.

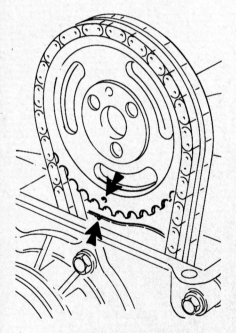

FIG 3•21 **KEEP MOVING PARTS RUNNING FREELY. OTHERWISE THEY'LL STICK AND STOP WORKING**

But if you're in a rut, a change of scene, neighbourhood and even friends can do you good. Beware the estate agent's patter, though. If they tell you a house 'has a lot of history, is in an area with a real sense of community and benefits from good transport links' you can rest assured that the previous owner was murdered there, that you'll soon know all the local junkies and winos by name, and that trains will be thundering past inches from your back door a dozen times an hour.

Going on holiday without each other
Again within reason, of course. A week playing golf in the Algarve or riding in Scotland, all-male and all-female respectively, is good. A weekend in Paris 'oh, just with the new guy at work, you don't know him, he's probably gay anyway or something' is not.

Mini-breaks
If you have children, beg, bribe or bludgeon (metaphorically, of course) grandparents or friends to look after them for a night or two so you can go away together. City centre hotels are often cheaper on weekends when the business crowd isn't staying.

⚠ Marriage DO'S and DON'TS

☑ **DO** forgive, frequently and often. Jesus said you should forgive seventy times seven, which at close on 500 times should see you through round about the first year of marriage. And if Jesus himself had been married he'd probably have popped a zero on the end of that figure.

☑ **DO** remember you're in this together. What you have and build together is – certainly should be – greater than either of you. There's a reason that humans throughout the worst times in history have found the basic survival unit to be not one but two. Except in the McLaren F1, which has three seats. But who can afford a McLaren F1 nowadays?

☑ **DO** grow. Not just laterally, though that'll probably happen too. Grow as a person and as a couple. This sounds awfully sincere and American and not at all British, where we like to pretend that only plants and bankers' bonuses grow, but it's true. You won't have the same beliefs and desires at 55 as you did at 25. Though you should still support the same football team.

☑ **DO** put things down. Such as the toilet seat and your mobile phone.

☑ **DO** celebrate the good things. Few things cause resentment faster than telling your spouse a piece of good news and have them ignore or belittle it. It may only be a thankyou letter from a client or the car service coming in cheaper than you'd thought, but even small victories are victories.

☑ **DO** pick things up. Such as your dirty clothes. And a bottle of red on the way home.

☒ **DON'T** cling to the romantic ideals you had while staring into your spouse's eyes on a Caribbean beach in front of all your family and friends. Life's no bowl of cherries.

☒ **DON'T** keep score. It's not a contest. Back rubs, emptying the dishwasher, taking the bins out, filling the car up – just do them without being asked.

Don't take everything too seriously. Things will seem better if you can laugh about them, and there's humour even in the bleakest circumstances.

Fault diagnosis

Fault	Diagnosis	Treatment
Husband can't find what he's looking for	It's right in front of him	Sigh deeply and point it out as though to a particularly stupid dog.
Wife falls asleep at 9.30 watching TV every night	She's exhausted and/or you're boring	If the latter is true then it's a bit late to fix it. Sorry.
Husband keeps tidying away objects in different places.	Tell him to – wait a sec. Your husband tidies stuff away?	Alert the media and set up a YouTube channel. This one's going viral.
Wife almost falls into toilet at 3am because he left the seat up	Husband is an inconsiderate jerk. So what's new?	A seat dropped hard will hurt any object caught between it and the toilet rim. You know what I'm saying here.
Mystery toothbrush in bathroom	It must belong to one of you.	Colour-code toothbrushes. Or get separate basins. Or even separate bathrooms.
Husband can't find favourite but daggy item of clothing	It has been 'disappeared' by a wife who could show the CIA a thing or two in this respect.	Let it go. Buy another item and begin the process of daggification all over again.
Wife running low on clean underwear	Wife needs clean underwear	Wife washes dirty underwear to make it clean.
Husband running low on clean underwear	Husband needs clean underwear	Husband buys new underwear.
Wife gets lost en route to her destination	Wife needs to find where she's going	Wife asks someone, gets correct information, arrives at the right place on time
Husband gets lost en route to his destination	Husband needs to find where he's going	Husband refuses to ask, becomes increasingly lost, is never seen again.

Conclusion

Marriage is tough. Whoever said it was a bed of roses was almost certainly unmarried (and probably not much of a gardener either). It may be that the secret to a lasting marriage is simply that both parties shouldn't want to get divorced at the same time.

There's no such thing as a perfect marriage. The best you can hope for is two imperfect people deciding to accept each other's imperfections – which is, as it turns out, a pretty good start. When your parents or grandparents point out that their generations in general stayed together longer than modern-day couples do, that may be something to do with it: that they weren't bombarded with expectations of the perfect marriage in the way people are nowadays. (Of course, many of them were deeply unhappy, and worse, too, and perhaps stayed together when in the long run they'd have been better off apart.)

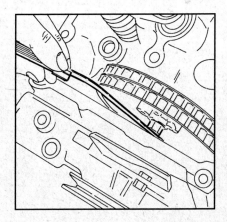

FIG 3•22 **FINE TUNING WILL BE REQUIRED**

There are no hard and fast rules to making your marriage work, other than the recognition that the meaning of the words 'hard' and 'fast' will gradually morph throughout your marriage: where once they meant sex they will eventually apply to Sudoku, having taken in work problems, home renovations and tax returns en route.

In marriage you are also building something both apart from either of you and bigger than either of you. Be proud of your spouse, in public as well as in private. Argue only behind closed doors. Beware of confiding in people outside your marriage unless you trust them implicitly. Don't sweat the small stuff, and you'll find that it's nearly all small stuff.

Above all, make each other laugh. Love and laughter go a long, long way.

Marriage is like a deck of cards. To start with, all you need is two hearts and a diamond. By the end, you'll wish you had a club and a spade.

Titles in the Haynes Explains series

Now that Haynes has explained Marriage, you can progress to our full size manuals on car maintenance (a little TLC will keep it running smoothly), *Lawnmower Manual* (the route to domestic bliss), *Women's Home DIY Manual* (because he'll be too busy mowing the lawn) and *Dance Manual* (a gentle transition from mosh to posh).

There are Haynes manuals on just about everything – but let us know if we've missed one.

Haynes.com